Quick & Easy PARTY CAKES

LINDSAY BRADSHAW

Many people buy a party cake purely because they don't have the time (or that's what they think) to make one. Obviously practised hands will be able to work more quickly than those less experienced. However, by taking a few short cuts, such as using good quality ready-made cake bases, working with covering paste renowned for its ease of use and creative possibilities, selecting readily available cake decorations and the minimum of specialist equipment, anyone can decorate and finish a cake in one hour - in fact, many cakes can be completed in much less time! This book will show you how to make an edible masterpiece to be proud of, giving you a real sense of satisfaction and achievement.

CONTENTS

JOLLY PIRATE

Any child will treasure memories of a party featuring this novel face cake, complete with spotted scarf and eye patch.

23 × 18cm (9 × 7in) oval sponge cake
buttercream or jam for filling and masking
410g (13oz) peachy-pink sugarpaste
140g (4½oz) purple sugarpaste
60g (2oz) each lemon and brown sugarpaste
45g (1½oz) each white and black sugarpaste

EQUIPMENT
28 × 23cm (11 × 9in) oval cake board
oval cutter

1 Split and sandwich the sponge cake with chosen filling and mask with buttercream or jam.

2 Reserving a little for the nose, roll out the peachy-pink sugarpaste and cover the cake. Place on the cake board.

3 Thinly roll out the purple paste. Gently flatten balls of lemon paste onto the purple paste to form a regular pattern. Continue rolling the paste to create a smooth, spotted 'material' effect. Attach to the top of the face for a scarf. Cut the trimmings to form a tied knot.

4 Make the eye, nose, mouth and eye patch and attach to the cake. For the tufts of hair, model short pointed shapes of brown paste.

Thinly roll out the purple paste and polish the surface to remove excess icing (confectioner's) sugar before applying the yellow balls for spots.

Use cutters to make the eyes from white and black paste; the nose is modelled as a small oval ball. Use templates for the mouth and eye patch.

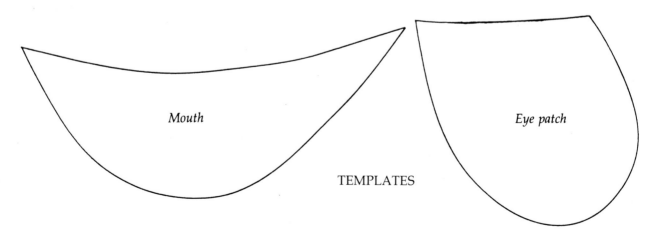

Mouth

Eye patch

TEMPLATES

YELLOW DINOSAUR

This multi-coloured species would certainly draw attention on a party table.

18cm (7in) round sponge cake
½ a small sponge layer or loaf cake
buttercream or jam for filling and masking
1.25kg (2½lb) lemon sugarpaste
60g (2oz) blue sugarpaste
280g (9oz) claret sugarpaste
22g (¾oz) each black and white sugarpaste

EQUIPMENT
45.5 × 20cm (18 × 8in) oblong cake board
130cm (52in) ribbon 7mm (¼in) wide for board edge

1 Split and sandwich the round sponge cake with chosen filling, then cut in half to form two semi-circles. Sandwich the two halves together, side by side, to form the basic body shape of the dinosaur. Shape the smaller cake into a cube for the head. Split and sandwich the cube of cake and arrange on the cake board with the body in a curved position. Mask the cake with buttercream or jam.

2 For the tail, take about 90g (3oz) of lemon sugarpaste and form a long carrot shape, attach to the body.

3 Reserve 125g (4oz) lemon paste, roll out the remaining paste and cover the cake. Place on the cake board. While still soft, indent the surface of the paste all over using the fingertips lightly pressed in.

4 Make balls of varying sizes from the blue sugarpaste, flatten and then press into the body and tail of the dinosaur.

5 Roll the claret paste into a long sausage and cut into pieces, graduating in size from small then large and back to small. Roll each piece into a ball, then shape into a squat carrot shape. Flatten the shape to form a spike. Repeat with each piece and attach to the body and tail in sequence of size.

6 For the legs, divide the remaining lemon paste into four pieces and shape as shown. Attach to the body.

7 Attach four flattened balls of yellow paste to the head, two for the eyes and two for the nostrils. Indent the nostrils with a fingertip. Roll the white paste into two ball shapes and attach to the eyes. Attach two smaller balls of black paste to the eyes. The mouth is made from a long thin strip of black paste attached to the head. Trim the cake board with ribbon.

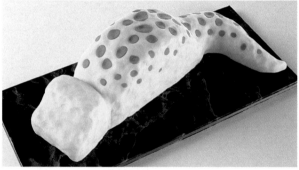

Cover the prepared cake shapes with yellow sugarpaste and create the interesting texture by indenting the surface with the fingertips.

Cut out pieces of claret sugarpaste in graduating sizes, roll into squat carrot shapes and flatten. Attach along the back and tail with water.

RAG DOLLY

This attractive birthday cake will be popular with little girls as they will love the hair and ribbon bows.

23 × 18cm (9 × 7in) oval sponge cake
buttercream or jam for filling and masking
345g (11oz) lemon sugarpaste
440g (14oz) peachy-pink sugarpaste
220g (7oz) brown sugarpaste
15g (½oz) each of deep peach, white, black and red
sugarpaste

EQUIPMENT
33 × 28cm (13 × 11in) oval cake board
crimping tool
paintbrush
2 ribbon bows

Use a template to cut out the two pieces of sugarpaste for the hair, marking the texture with the rounded tip of a paintbrush handle.

1 Split and sandwich the sponge cake with chosen filling and mask with buttercream or jam.

2 Roll out the lemon sugarpaste and use to cover the cake board, then crimp the edge with the crimping tool while the paste is still soft.

3 Roll out the peachy-pink sugarpaste and cover the cake. Place on the prepared board.

4 Roll out the brown sugarpaste and use the template on page 39 to cut out two hair shapes. Texture with the tip of a paintbrush handle. Make two plaits from the remaining paste as shown. Attach all parts to the cake.

5 Prepare the eyes, nose, mouth and cheeks as shown on page 39 and attach to the face. Pipe in some eyelashes if liked. Attach a ribbon bow to each plait with a dab of icing.

Cut out the eyes and cheeks from coloured sugarpaste and a long thin rope of red paste for the mouth. Model a small oval ball for the nose.

CUTE TEDDY

Always popular, this friendly teddy bear cake could be used for children's birthdays and christening celebrations.

1 large sphere-shaped sponge cake
1 medium sphere-shaped sponge cake
buttercream or jam for filling and masking
1.375kg (2¾lb) tan sugarpaste
reconstituted egg white
small amount of royal icing
30g (1oz) brown sugarpaste
7g (¼oz) black sugarpaste
22g (¾oz) black royal icing
peach dusting powder (blossom tint)

EQUIPMENT
30 × 25cm (12 × 10in) oval cake board
1 plastic cake pillar dowel (optional)
dusting brush
no. 2 piping tube (tip)
1 large ribbon bow

1 Split and sandwich the two sphere-shaped cakes with the chosen filling. The medium-sized cake may be left round, or you may prefer to sculpt the cake to more of an oval shape. Use a sharp knife dipped into warm water to make clean cuts. Chilling or part-freezing the cake prior to shaping makes the task easier. Mask each cake separately with buttercream or jam.

2 Roll out separate circles of tan sugarpaste and cover each prepared cake, smoothing the paste with the palms of your hands to create a neat finish. Attach the head to the body with reconstituted egg white or, to ensure that the cake is firmly attached, you may prefer to insert a plastic cake pillar dowel into the body and then push the head onto the dowel. Position on the cake board.

After shaping the cakes and spreading with buttercream, cover each shape with tan-coloured sugarpaste, then position the head on the body.

3 Shape two arms and two legs from the remaining paste and stick to the body with royal icing. Thinly roll out the brown-coloured paste and cut out two circles, attach to the legs as shown.

4 Thickly roll out some more tan paste and cut out a circle. Cut the circle in half and indent each with your thumb to form two ears. Stick them on to the head.

5 Using the dusting brush, apply a light blush of dusting powder to the cheeks as shown. It is a good idea to make a temporary 'bib' of absorbent kitchen paper for the teddy to catch any falling dusting powder that may otherwise stain the body.

6 Make two small flat circles of black sugarpaste for the eyes and a small oval for the nose, attach to the face. Pipe the mouth and stitching using a no. 2 tube (tip) with black royal icing. Attach the bow to the teddy's neck.

Shape the legs and arms from tan-coloured sugarpaste. While still pliable, attach to the body with dabs of tan-coloured royal icing or softened sugarpaste.

To prevent falling dusting powder settling on the sugarpaste surface, it is advisable to tuck a kitchen paper 'bib' under the teddy's neck.

RED AEROPLANE

A colourful novelty cake that will suit boys or aspiring pilots of all ages. Change the colours to suit the recipient.

500g (1lb) sponge loaf
buttercream or jam for filling and masking
315g (10oz) blue sugarpaste
125g (4oz) white sugarpaste
280g (9oz) red sugarpaste
15g (½oz) black sugarpaste
7g (¼oz) egg yellow sugarpaste
1 modelled marzipan or plastic pilot figure

EQUIPMENT
28cm (11in) cake board
oval cutter
small piece each red and black card
61cm (44in) ribbon for board edge

1 Roll out the blue sugarpaste and cover the cake board. Roll out the white paste to the same thickness as used to cover the board. Use the cloud template to cut out shapes from the blue paste in a random fashion over the board. Replace the removed blue with white cloud and smooth the joins with the fingers.

2 Using a sharp knife dipped in warm water, shape the sponge loaf as shown to form the body of the aeroplane. To make cutting easier and neater, chill or part-freeze the cake prior to shaping. Remove the cockpit using the oval cutter. Mask the cake shape with buttercream or jam.

3 Roll out 200g (6½oz) red paste and cover the body shape, trim the base and smooth the paste with the palms of the hands to create a neat finish. Place the cake across the board.

4 Make templates of the two wing shapes. Roll out the remaining red paste and cut out two of each wing shape. Attach to the aeroplane and board. Trace the tail shape onto red card and cut out neatly. Join to the aeroplane by gently inserting into the soft paste at the narrow end of the body

and the small rear wings. Roll out the black paste and cut out six small ovals for the windows. Position on the cake.

5 Make a tracing of the propeller on thin black card and cut out. Shape a flat circle of egg yellow paste. Attach both pieces to the aeroplane with dabs of icing. Sit the modelled marzipan or plastic pilot figure in the cockpit. Trim the cake board with ribbon.

After covering the board with blue paste, use the template to cut out cloud shapes which are then replaced with cut-out shapes of white sugarpaste.

Use a sharp bladed knife dipped into warm water to shape the body of the aeroplane. Remove a small oval of sponge for the cockpit using a cutter.

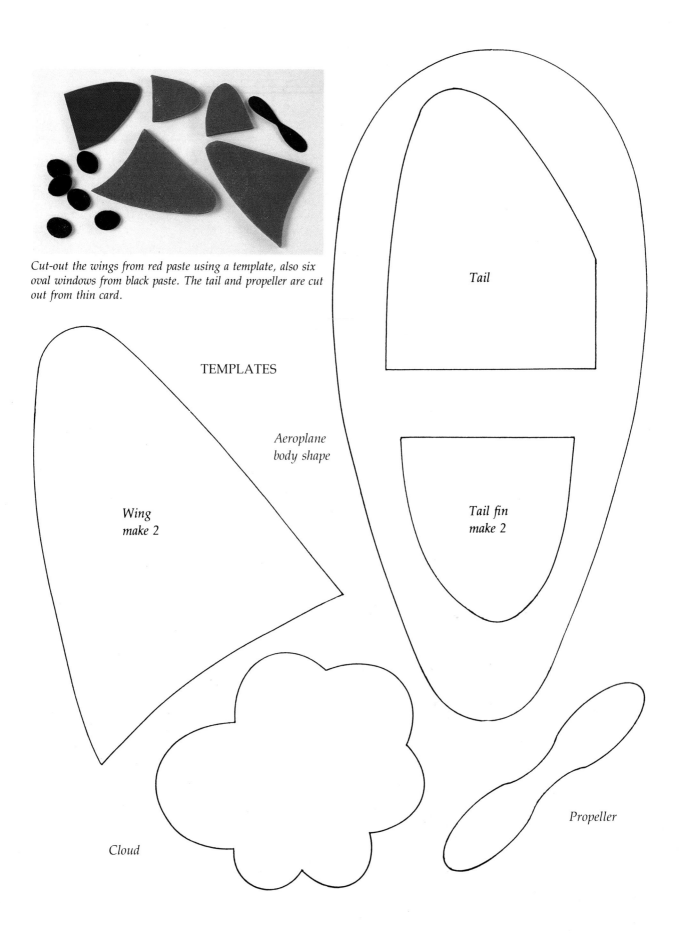

Cut-out the wings from red paste using a template, also six oval windows from black paste. The tail and propeller are cut out from thin card.

TEMPLATES

Tail

Aeroplane
body shape

Wing
make 2

Tail fin
make 2

Cloud

Propeller

GREY RABBIT

Both girls and boys would welcome the friendly smile of this cheerful rabbit at their birthday party.

20 × 15cm (8 × 6in) oval sponge cake
13cm (5in) shallow round sponge cake
buttercream or jam for filling and masking
470g (15oz) grey sugarpaste
345g (11oz) white sugarpaste
100g (3½oz) pink sugarpaste
45g (1½oz) each brown, black, red and peachy-pink
sugarpaste
60g (2oz) black royal icing

EQUIPMENT
45.5 × 30cm (18 × 12in) oblong cake board
no. 3 piping tube (tip)

1 Cut the oval sponge cake in half and sandwich with filling. Cut the small round cake into two semi-circles and sandwich with filling to make one deep semi-circle. Trim the cake to the same height as the oval cake and join together with buttercream or jam, as shown on page 16.

2 Use 220g (7oz) grey sugarpaste to cover the top part of the cake and cover the lower part with white sugarpaste, making a neat join where the two colours meet. Shape the grey paste at the join as shown in the main photo.

3 Roll out the remaining grey sugarpaste and use the template to cut out two ear shapes. Attach the ears to the head with water. Roll out the pink sugarpaste quite thinly and use a smaller template to cut out the inner ears. Attach to the grey ears with water. Bend over the tip of one grey ear.

4 Roll out the various colours of sugarpaste quite thinly and, using templates, cut out the various eyes, mouth, teeth and tongue shapes. Model a nose from the peachy-pink paste. Attach the pieces to the face with water. Using a no. 3 tube (tip) with black royal icing, pipe the outline of the mouth, the whiskers and eyebrows.

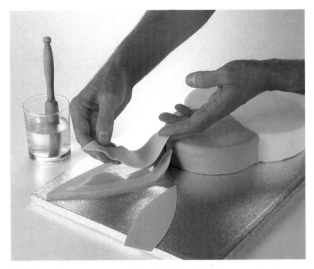

Roll out the grey paste quite thickly and use a template to cut out the ear shapes. The pink inlays use a smaller template and are attached with water.

Thinly roll out some white, black and pink sugarpaste and use templates to make the eyes and mouth. Shape a pointed ball of pink for the nose.

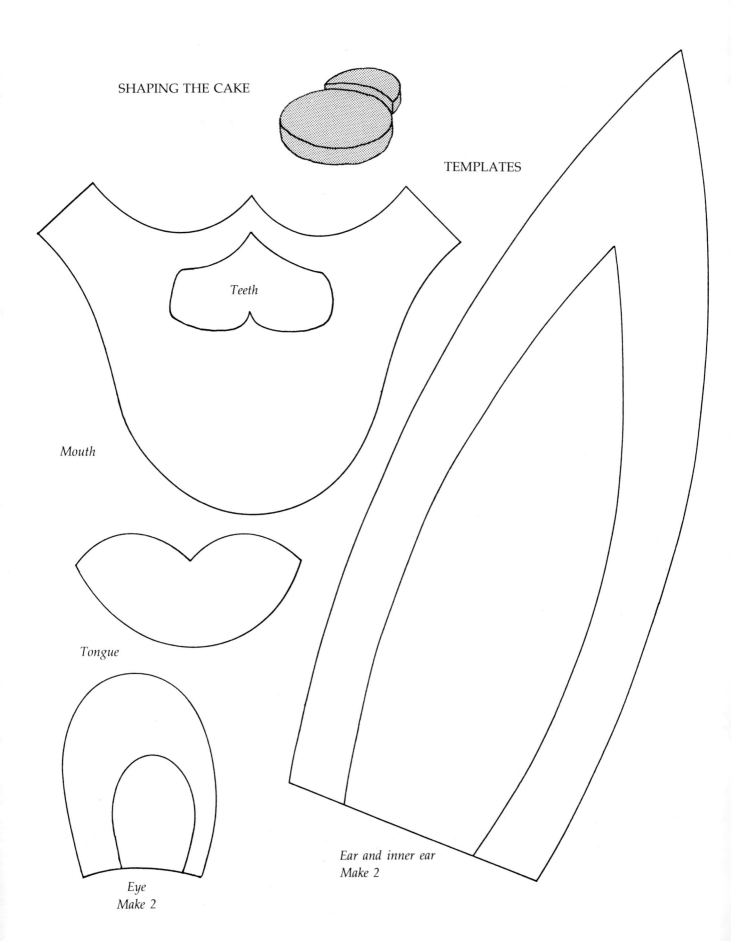

SHAPING THE CAKE

TEMPLATES

Teeth

Mouth

Tongue

Eye
Make 2

Ear and inner ear
Make 2

16

BIRTHDAY EXPRESS

A dream come true for any young child hoping to be a train driver.

20cm (8in) square sponge cake
small jam-filled Swiss roll
buttercream or jam for filling and masking
470g (15oz) navy sugarpaste
185g (6oz) black sugarpaste
45g (1½oz) yellow sugarpaste
60g (2oz) each red, grey and white sugarpaste
60g (2oz) royal icing

EQUIPMENT
30 × 20cm (12 × 8in) oblong cake board
assorted round cutters
gold plastic bell
2 plastic 'Happy Birthday' writings
coloured sweets

1 Cut the sponge in half and sandwich with filling. Cut out as shown on page 18 and assemble to form the basic shape, joining the parts together with buttercream or jam.

2 Cover the prepared engine shape with navy sugarpaste and position on cake board ready for decoration.

3 Cut the Swiss roll to the required length, about 9cm (3½in). If necessary, unroll the cake until the desired diameter of about 5.5cm (2¼in) is obtained. Cover the Swiss roll with navy sugarpaste and attach to the engine with royal icing.

Use a sharp knife dipped into warm water to cut out the cake shapes. Sandwich with the chosen filling and assemble as shown.

Spread the small Swiss roll with buttercream or jam and position on a rolled out strip of blue sugarpaste. Roll up and neaten the join.

4 Roll out the black sugarpaste to a thickness of about 2.5mm (⅛in) and cut out a rectangle to form the roof, allowing about 5mm (¼in) overhang all the way around the roof. Attach to the cabin with royal icing.

5 Roll out the remaining black sugarpaste to a thickness of 1cm (⅜in) and cut out eight small wheels and two large wheels. Roll out the grey sugarpaste to a similar thickness and cut out two long bar shapes, see page 48. Roll out the yellow sugarpaste and cut out the window shapes and the front plate. The boiler front is a circle of red sugarpaste, with the remaining red used to model the funnel.

6 Attach the various parts to the train with royal icing, waiting a few minutes to allow each part to set a little.

7 Attach the coloured sweets to the front of the train with royal icing and to each wheel, as shown. Attach the plastic bell behind the funnel and finish the cake with the plastic 'Happy Birthday' writings, attached to each side of the boiler with royal icing.

Roll out the various colours of sugarpaste and use cutters and templates to prepare the wheels, axles, window, roof and boiler front.

> **NOTE**
> As there are a lot of off-pieces and shapes to make for this cake, a short cut could be to use large sweets or shop-bought chocolate or icing-covered biscuits for the wheels.

SHAPING THE CAKE

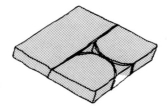

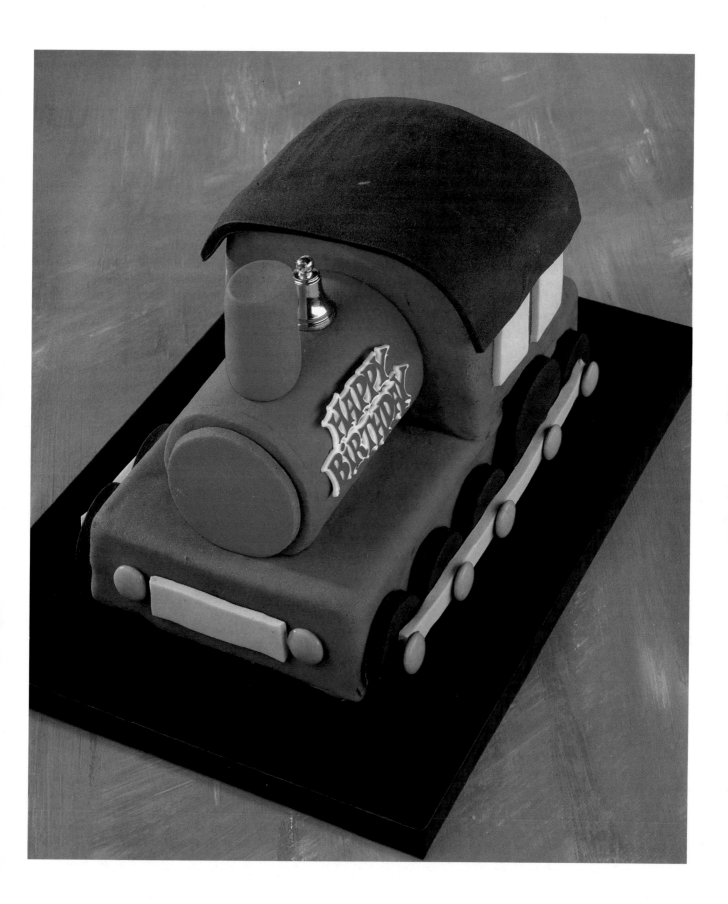

GREEN MONSTER

Not too frightening! This novelty cake would make an ideal centrepiece for a children's theme party.

15cm (6in) shallow round sponge cake
15cm (6in) square sponge cake
buttercream or jam for filling and masking
345g (11oz) green sugarpaste
60g (2oz) navy sugarpaste
30g (1oz) each white and black sugarpaste
30g (1oz) black royal icing

EQUIPMENT
30 × 25cm (12 × 10in) oblong cake board
paintbrush
oval cutter (optional)
round cutter (optional)
no. 2 piping tube (tip)

1 Cut the round sponge in half and sandwich with filling. Split the square cake and sandwich with filling. Join the cakes as shown on page 22 and mask with buttercream or jam. Cover the prepared shape with green sugarpaste and place on the cake board.

2 Using the template, cut out the hair from navy sugarpaste and attach to the head. Texture the hair with lines using the tip of a paintbrush handle.

3 Cut out the ears and shape the nose as shown from the green sugarpaste trimmings. Prepare the eyes, teeth and mouth from the white and black sugarpaste. Attach all parts to the cake with water. Pipe an outline around the eyes and corners of the mouth with the no. 2 tube (tip) and black royal icing.

Use a card template to cut out the hair shape. The hair texture is created by making indented lines, using the rounded tip of a paintbrush handle.

Make the eyes, nose, mouth and teeth by cutting the shapes from thinly rolled sugarpaste with the aid of templates; use a cutter for the ears.

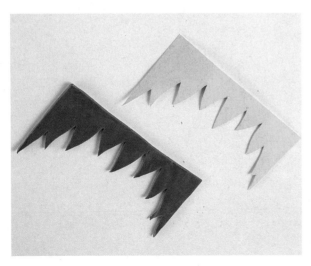

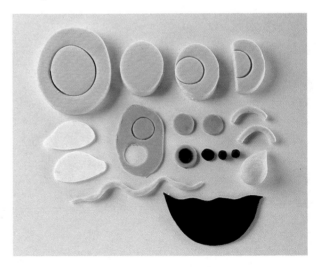

SHAPING THE CAKE

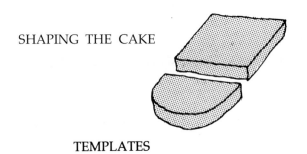

TEMPLATES

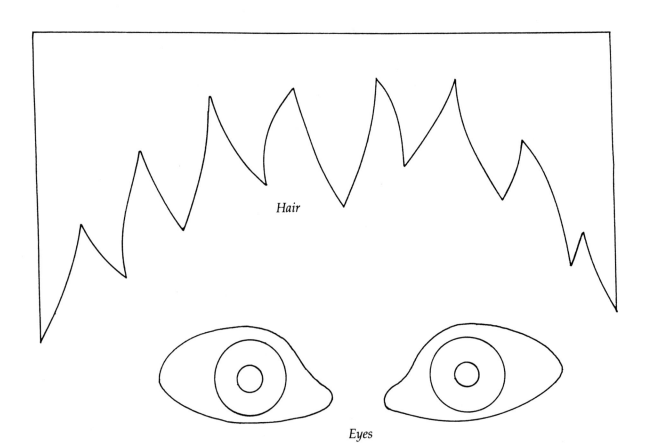

Hair

Eyes

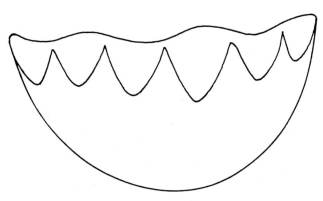

Mouth and teeth

MICE IN A BASKET

These two mice snug in a basket would make a lovely birthday cake for twins.

18cm (7in) round sponge cake
buttercream or jam for filling and masking
250g (8oz) chocolate sugarpaste
375g (12oz) coffee sugarpaste
185g (6oz) grey sugarpaste
15g (½oz) black sugarpaste
125g (4oz) pink sugarpaste
30g (1oz) royal icing

EQUIPMENT
25cm (10in) round cake board
basketweave rolling pin
string
ball modelling tool
no. 2 piping tube (tip)
about 90cm (1yd) ribbon for cake side and bow
about 90cm (1yd) ribbon for board edge

1 Cut the sponge cake in half and sandwich with filling. Spread the top and sides with masking material. Roll out chocolate sugarpaste and cover the cake. Place the covered cake on the cake board, positioning it slightly off-centre.

2 Roll out the coffee sugarpaste quite thickly and texture the surface with the basketweave rolling pin. Ensure that the paste is long enough to fit around the cake – measure the cake with string to give you an idea of the length required. Use a scalloped template to cut out the shape, moving the template along the paste to complete. Attach the piece to the cake side with water, neatening the join at the back of the cake.

3 Model the mice heads from the grey sugarpaste by making a large, pointed pear shape for each and, while the paste is still soft, indent the eyes using a ball modelling tool. Roll two ball shapes for the ears and press on a smaller ball of pink paste

Thickly roll out the light brown sugarpaste, texture with a basketweave rolling pin and scallop the edge using a template as a guide. Attach to the cake.

Model the heads from grey sugarpaste and pipe the eyes using white and black royal icing. Use a cocktail stick (toothpick) to make whisker marks.

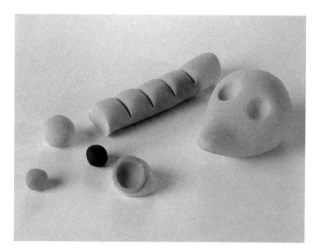

for the inner ear. Using the modelling tool, indent both together to create the finished ear. Attach the ears to the head with water. Using a no. 2 tube (tip) with white royal icing, pipe the eyes on, then roll two tiny balls of black sugarpaste and position on the eyes. Roll out two larger balls of black sugarpaste for the noses and attach in position with water.

4 Attach the ribbon and bow around the cake sides, ensuring that the bow is positioned at the front. Gather up any sugarpaste trimmings, knead together and model two pear shapes similar to those made for the heads but slightly smaller, attach the pieces to the cake top and press gently to flatten slightly – these will represent the bodies of the mice.

5 Roll out the pink sugarpaste quite thinly and cut out an 18cm (7in) circle, using a template, dinner plate or other suitable guide. Moisten the top area of the cake and the mice bodies and lay the circle on top, allowing it to find its own level. Fix the edges around the mouse heads to make them appear to be peeping from beneath. Attach ribbon to the board edge.

Thinly roll out some pink sugarpaste and use a template to cut out the large circle. Attach to the cake while still pliable.

BOX OF CHOCS

This luxurious edible box of confections must be a chocaholics dream; alter the inscription to suit the occasion.

18cm (7in) square chocolate sponge cake
buttercream for filling and masking
440g (14oz) ivory pastillage
200g (6½oz) black sugarpaste
125g (4oz) red pastillage
185g (6oz) chocolate, melted
30g (1oz) black royal icing
assortment of luxury chocolates

EQUIPMENT
28cm (11in) square cake board
ribbed rolling pin
no. 1, 4 and 43 piping tubes (tip)
10cm (4in) gold thread
1.25m (1⅓yd) ribbon for board edge and bow

1 Roll out the black sugarpaste and cover the cake board. Cut the cake in half and sandwich with filling. Make a 15cm (6in) square template from thin card or paper and place centrally on top of the sponge cake. Use a sharp knife to champher the cake at an angle from the template edge to the outside base edge of the cake. Reserve the template for use later in step 2. Spread the top and sides with buttercream and place on the prepared cake board.

2 Make a template of the cake side shape and size. Roll out the ivory pastillage and texture the surface using the ribbed rolling pin. Cut out four side shapes, ensuring the ribbing runs in the same direction on all four sides. Attach to the cake and if possible, try to extend the sides about 5mm (¼in) above the height of the cake to create a box effect. Also cut out a square lid from the textured paste using the cake cutting template. Again, reserve the template.

3 Roll out the ivory pastillage trimmings thinly and cut out a rectangle for the gift tag. Cut a hole in the tag using a no. 4 tube (tip).

4 Add a few drops of cold water to the melted chocolate to thicken it slightly. Using a no. 43 tube (tip) with the prepared chocolate, pipe a shell border around the top and base edges and corners of the box. Pipe around the edge of the box lid.

5 Using a no. 1 tube with black royal icing, pipe an inscription of your choice onto the prepared gift tag. Knot the gold thread through the hole.

6 Roll out very thinly the red pastillage and cut out a square using the reserved template. Lay the square crossways on top of the cake to look like tissue paper lining. Arrange the chocolates in the box and attach the prepared gift tag and pink bow with melted chocolate. Trim the cake board edge with ribbon.

Roll out thickly the ivory-coloured sugarpaste and use a template to cut out the tapered edge strips which are then attached to the cake sides.

For the gift tag, roll out thinly some ivory sugarpaste and cut out a small oblong. Use a tube (tip) to make a hole for the tie and pipe on the inscription.

LET'S PARTY

Get in the party mood with this brightly coloured cake which, with a change of numerals, can be adapted for any age.

23 × 18cm (9 × 7in) oval sponge cake
buttercream or jam for filling and masking
750g (1½lb) lemon sugarpaste
90g (3oz) chocolate sugarpaste
30g (1oz) each white, red, yellow and blue pastillage
125g (4oz) yellow royal icing
30g (1oz) black royal icing
gold and silver edible food colouring

EQUIPMENT
33 × 28cm (13 × 11in) oval board
small oval cutter
small and medium star cutters
small alphabet cutters
large number cutters
no. 1 and 3 piping tubes (tips)
assorted colours of narrow gift or florists' ribbon
scissors
1m (1yd 3in) ribbon for board edge

1 Roll out thinly red, yellow and blue pastillage and cut out 15 oval shapes for balloons. Roll out white pastillage and cut out five small and five medium stars. Set aside on a flat surface to firm up.

For the balloons, roll out thinly some bright colours of pastillage paste and use a small oval cutter to make the shapes.

2 Roll out thinly the chocolate sugarpaste and use the small and large alphabet and number cutters to prepare the desired inscription, set the letters aside. Paint the prepared stars with gold and silver food colouring.

3 Cut the sponge cake and sandwich with filling. Mask the top and sides with buttercream or jam. Cover the cake with lemon sugarpaste. Cover the cake board with lemon sugarpaste and place the cake on top. Using tube (tip) no. 3 with yellow royal icing pipe a plain shell border around the base of the cake.

4 Attach the prepared lettering to the cake top with a little water or use tiny dabs of royal icing. Attach the balloons in groups of three around the cake side and the prepared stars with dabs of royal icing. Tilt the cake very carefully on a small box or other suitable object and using a no. 1 tube (tip) with black royal icing, pipe the balloon strings.

5 Cut the gift ribbon into short lengths and curl by pulling tightly against the blunt side of a scissor blade. Attach the ribbon curls with dabs of royal icing. Cover the board edge with ribbon.

Roll out some pastillage paste quite thinly and use a small star cutter to make the shapes. Paint the stars with edible gold and silver colour.

BLACK AND WHITE CAKE

Something different . . . this cake could be used as a centrepiece for a party table for any adult celebration.

20cm (8in) square rich fruit cake covered with marzipan (almond paste)
clear alcohol (gin or vodka)
575g (1lb 2½oz) white sugarpaste
105g (3½oz) black sugarpaste
30g (1oz) grey royal icing
150 silver dragees
pink foil-covered chocolate spheres

EQUIPMENT
28cm (11in) square cake board
no. 1 piping tube (tip)
30cm (12in) ribbon for champagne glass
champagne glass

1 Reserve 60g (2oz) each of white and black sugarpaste. Divide the white into two pieces and shape into a rough oblong, shape the black into an oblong and sandwich between the two pieces of white. Roll up Swiss-roll fashion and cut into slices. Group the pieces together in a random

fashion and roll out to give a streaky, marbled effect. Brush the cake with alcohol and cover with the prepared paste. Trim away any excess paste from the edges and place the cake centrally on the cake board.

2 Take the reserved white and black sugarpaste and roll each out into two long narrow ropes, twist together and roll slightly to neaten. Attach the twisted rope to the base of the cake with water, trim and join neatly at the back of the cake.

3 Using a no. 1 tube (tip) with grey royal icing, pipe random groups of three small dots and single dots over the top and sides of the cake, attaching a silver dragee to each dot. Pipe a few at a time otherwise the icing may dry before you have attached the dragee.

4 Tie the ribbon in a bow around the stem of the champagne glass. Position the glass in the centre of the cake and pile with pink foil-wrapped chocolate spheres.

Take similar amounts of white and black sugarpaste and roll out slightly. Layer together, then roll up Swiss roll fashion ready to use.

Roll a long narrow sausage of white and black sugarpaste and twist together to form a neatly striped border. Attach to the cake with water.

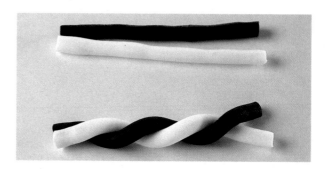

ANNIVERSARY BELL

Shaped cake tins are now widely available – try a bell shape to make a stunning cake for a Golden Anniversary.

1 medium-size bell-shaped rich fruit cake covered with marzipan (almond paste)
clear alcohol
440g (14oz) egg yellow sugarpaste
30g (1oz) ivory sugarpaste
30g (1oz) royal icing

EQUIPMENT
20cm (8in) round gold cake board
23cm (9in) round gold cake board
25cm (10in) round gold cake board
2.5m (3yd) gold banding
double-sided adhesive tape
crimper
oval cutter
no. 1 piping tube (tip)
18cm (7in) strung gold beads
gold plastic 50 numeral
plastic posy spike
wired crescent spray of yellow fabric flowers, gold leaves and ribbon loops

1 Trim the edges of each cake board with gold banding and attach them together in a tiered fashion using double-sided tape. Brush the cake with alcohol and cover with egg yellow sugarpaste, trim away the excess paste and place the cake on the prepared stepped cake boards. Make a decorative edge as shown around the lower part of the bell using a crimper while the paste is still soft.

2 Roll out the ivory sugarpaste and cut out an oval shape. Using a no. 1 tube (tip) with royal icing, pipe a line around the edge of the oval shape and attach the gold beads, pressing gently into place. Attach the plastic numeral with tiny dabs of icing and attach the finished plaque to the cake with royal icing.

3 Push the plastic posy spike into the top of the cake and insert the wired flower arrangement and the ribbon loops, securing with a plug of sugarpaste.

Cover the cake with marzipan and sugarpaste and position on the prepared stepped cake boards. While the paste is soft, use a crimper to make a fancy edging.

Thinly roll out some ivory pastillage and cut out an oval shape. Using no. 2 tube, pipe a line on the edge and attach the gold beads as shown.

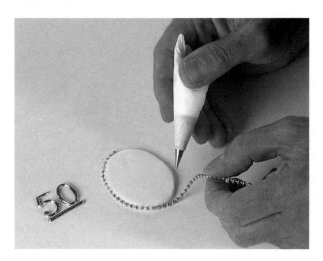

PEACH DRAGEE CAKE

The gold dragees just add a special sparkle to this delicately coloured cake suitable for any occasion.

20cm (8in) hexagonal rich fruit cake covered with marzipan (almond paste)
60g (2oz/¼ cup) boiled apricot jam
125g (4oz) marzipan (almond paste)
clear alcohol (gin or vodka)
625g (1¼lb) peach sugarpaste
about 100 gold dragees
60g (2oz) peach royal icing

EQUIPMENT
25cm (10in) hexagonal cake board
plastic ruler
nos. 1 and 2 piping tubes (tips)
tweezers (optional)
about 90cm (1yd) ribbon for board edge
about 90cm (1yd) lace for board edge
wired spray of peach flowers and ribbon loops

1 Use the ruler to indent lines from point to point on the cake top by pressing gently. Take a sharp knife and neatly cut any one of the six sections and remove the wedge to leave a space. The removed wedge can be sliced and wrapped to make extra portions. Brush the exposed cut surfaces of the fruit cake with apricot jam and cover with the rolled out marzipan, neatening the joins and edges.

2 Brush the marzipan with alcohol and cover the cake with peach sugarpaste. Whilst the sugarpaste is still soft, mark the quiltwork pattern with the ruler on the top and sides of the cake as shown in the photo.

3 Using a no. 1 tube (tip) pipe tiny dots of royal icing where the quiltwork lines cross and attach a gold dragee on each – if you find the dragees difficult to pick up and position, use tweezers. Position the dragees before the icing sets.

4 Roll out the remaining peach sugarpaste to cover the cake board, position the cake and trim the board edge with ribbon and lace. Pipe a small, plain shell border around the base of the cake using a no. 2 tube (tip) with peach royal icing. Attach the spray of flowers in the cut away area with a spot of royal icing.

Immediately after covering the cake, and while the paste is still soft, mark the diagonal quilt pattern using a ruler or royal icing smoother.

Using a no. 1 tube (tip) with peach royal icing, pipe a tiny dab of icing into each cross of the quilting. Attach the dragees using tweezers.

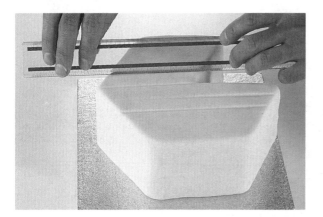

HAPPY NEW YEAR

Rich colours and a traditional thistle decoration make a spectacular cake to cut when the clock strikes midnight.

25 × 20cm (10 × 8in) oval rich fruit cake covered with marzipan (almond paste)
clear alcohol (gin or vodka)
750g (1½lb) claret sugarpaste
250g (8oz) deep green sugarpaste
60g (2oz) white sugarpaste
60g (2oz) royal icing
30g (1oz) black royal icing
wired spray of fabric eryngium thistles, small and large berries and ribbon loops

EQUIPMENT
33cm (13in) round cake board
1m (1yd 3in) ribbon for board edge
68cm (27in) tartan ribbon
scriber or hat pin
no. 1 piping tube (tip)
small piece of gold card

1 Roll out deep green sugarpaste and cover cake board. Brush cake with clear alcohol and roll out claret sugarpaste. Cover the cake in the conventional manner and place slightly off-centre on the prepared cake board. Trim the cake board edge with ribbon and position tartan ribbon around the base of the cake, join and secure at the back of the cake with a dab of royal icing.

2 Roll out the white sugarpaste thinly and, using a template, cut out the oval clock face shape. Attach to the right-hand side of the cake top with water. Make a tracing of the inscription and position on cake top, pin-prick each letter onto sugarpaste covering. Using a no. 1 tube (tip) with royal icing slightly softened with a few drops of cold water, pipe on the inscription.

Cover the cake with marzipan and claret sugarpaste in the conventional manner. Position the cake on the dark green sugarpasted cake board.

Position the tartan ribbon around the base of the cake, join and secure at the back of the cake with a dab of royal icing.

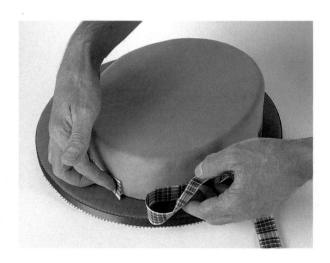

3 Using a no. 1 tube with black royal icing, pipe the numerals on the clock face and edge the oval shape with a scalloped line. Cut out the clock hands from gold card and attach to the clock with a dab of icing. Position the wired flower and foliage spray and attach to the cake board with royal icing.

Make a tracing of the lettering and use a scriber to pin-prick the design onto the cake. Pipe on the inscription.

TEMPLATE   *Clock face*

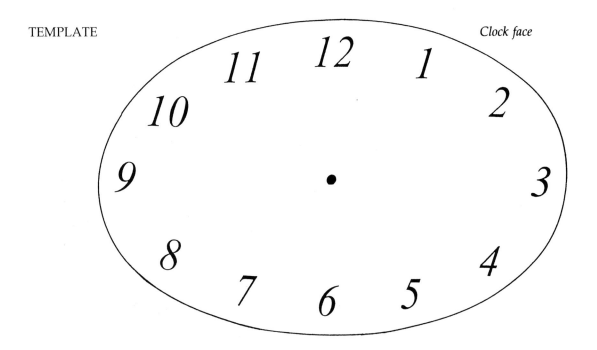

Lettering

$\mathcal{H}appy\ \mathcal{N}ew\ \mathcal{Y}ear$

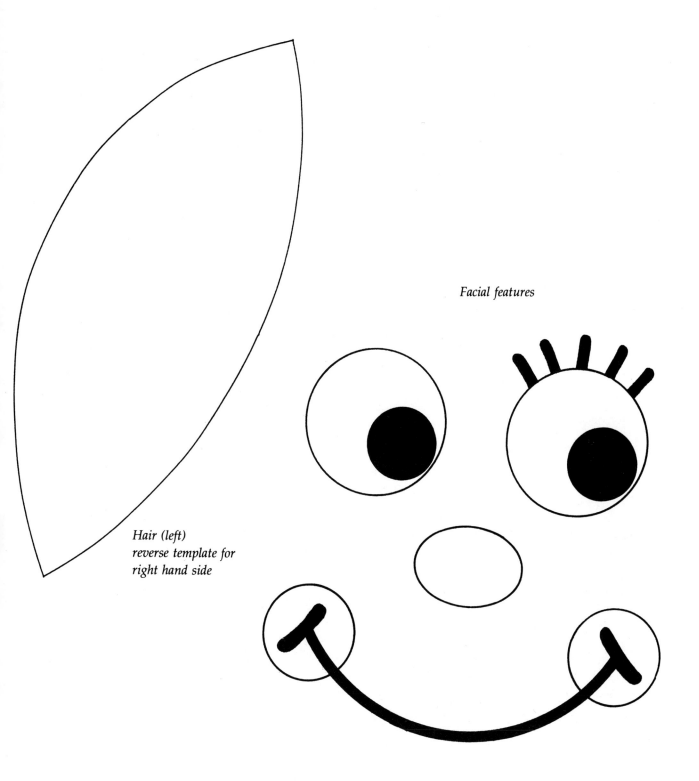

Facial features

Hair (left)
reverse template for
right hand side

EQUIPMENT

For some people, the commercial 'bandwagon' has spoiled their cake decorating, especially when they are told by a teacher or sales assistant that they really need specialist tools and equipment, and that a particular technique cannot be carried out without it. I go along with this in many cases, and having the right tools for the job in hand does make life easier. However, with a little thought and selectiveness, you can save yourself considerable expense and a kitchen drawer full of redundant items that you may only use once.

I have purposely designed the majority of cakes in the book to require the minimum of special equipment and most only require basic kitchen items that you probably already have, such as a rolling pin, small knife, palette knife, cutting board and pastry brush. When special items of equipment are specified in the list, please don't immediately dash out and buy them. More often than not you can use or at least adapt another item from the kitchen cupboard or technique to achieve a similar effect. Here are just a few such adaptations that may inspire you and will certainly save you money.

Tool	*Alternative*
Garrett frill cutter	Use a large scone cutter or fluted round cutter.
Rib rolling pin	Roll out sugarpaste and indent equally spaced parallel lines using a plastic ruler.
Broderie cutter	Create the desired pattern combination of holes using a No. 2, 3 or 4 plain writing tube (tip).
Clay gun	Roll out the sugarpaste thinly or in ropes, then twist and/or cut to create the desired shape.
Cutters	Simply draw or trace the required shape onto thin card and cut out to use as a template to cut around.
Sphere tin	Bake the cake in a pudding basin and when cool, sculpt to a rounder shape using a sharp knife dipped in warm water.
Ball modelling tool	Make a similar tool by sanding the blunt end of a wooden meat skewer to make a rounded shape.

You will probably already have most of the tools and equipment required to make the cakes in this book in your kitchen drawer. A few of the cakes require special items, as shown here.

BASIC EQUIPMENT

For the majority of finishes shown on the cakes in this book you will need the following basic equipment to get started:

Cutting board
Rolling pin
Small knife for cutting shapes and trimming
Medium-sized palette knife
Small brush
Icing sugar for dusting when rolling

Although a turntable does make it easier to manoeuvre the cake whilst decorating it, it is not essential for the cakes featured.

If you do get hooked by cake decorating, which is likely as it is quite addictive, be very selective when you shop and only buy those items that are essential to your work. As you progress, your experienced eye will soon establish that many cutters and tools have more than one use.

CAKE BOARDS

As a way of incorporating more colour and interest to your finished cake, with the minimum of work, you should try some of the board-covering ideas featured in this book. Covering the cake board with decorative paper still creates an attractive, finished look to your creation but eliminates the need to cover the board with sugarpaste and probably crimp the edges, and you will have realised already that the former method is less expensive.

Though the recipes suggest a particular board finish, you can quite easily change it to suit your own preferences and the time you have available. To cover a board with paper, simply cut the chosen paper about 3cm (1¼in) larger than the actual board. If using decorative gift wrapping paper, you will need to glue it to the board using a non-toxic glue (the stick-type ones are usually the best for this job). Self-adhesive laminate, the type used for shelves and covering books, is not as messy as glue can be and is certainly easier to work with. Turn the paper neatly over the board edge and secure on the reverse side of the board. For round and other curved shapes, pull and pleat the paper as you go around the board to create a neat finish.

Shop around in stationers, card and gift shops to find the nicest papers – you will enjoy matching and co-ordinating the coverings to the cake and you can create exactly the look you wish from stripy, spotty, flowery or sophisticated papers.

If time and your budget allows, give your covered cake boards an extra special touch by edging with gold or silver banding or satin or velvet ribbon. Each can be quickly and cleanly attached using a non-toxic stick-type adhesive or a narrow length of double-sided adhesive tape.

Cake boards can be used as they are or, for a more attractive finish, cover them with decorative foils or gift wrapping paper and trim the edge with banding or ribbon.

COMMERCIALLY AVAILABLE INGREDIENTS AND DECORATIONS

To get the greatest benefit from the quick-to-decorate concept, you really should cut out the fuss and buy in as much ready-made material and decoration as you can without sacrificing every bit of hand-crafted work and making the cake look cheap or mass-produced. Use what time you have available to actually cover, quickly dress and trim the cake, almost instantly, rather than spending hours mixing your own sugarpaste, making flowers and doing lots of laborious decoration. For fun and novelty cakes certainly, you'll probably find the last-minute or impulse cakes are more stunning than those planned in advance, and more importantly you'll also have more fun doing them!

SUGARPASTE

With the standard of consistent product, improved flavour and wide range of ready-coloured pastes now available in sugarcraft shops and supermarkets, it really isn't worth weighing ingredients, warming and mixing your own. You can buy sugarpaste in

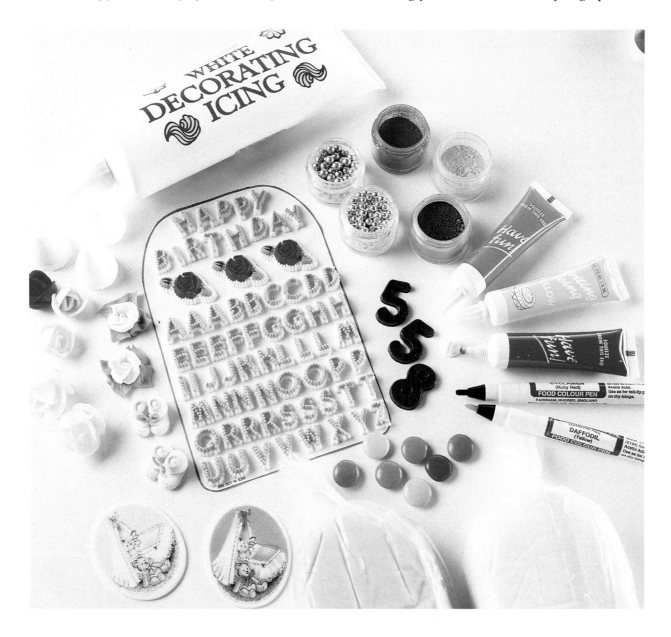

white and a host of useful pale tints and also in strong colours – even black – so there's something suitable for all occasions. The sugarpaste is conveniently packed in small retail packs. If, however, you use a lot, you may be able to negotiate a good discount for bulk buying.

PASTILLAGE

Just a few of the recipes in the book need pastillage – a hard-setting paste used for modelling. Again, it really isn't worth making your own. Buy an instant dry mix type that you simply mix with water. Alternatively, for its uses in this book, you could knead 1 tsp gum tragacanth powder into 500g (1lb) sugarpaste.

DECORATIONS

The increased interest in cake decoration over the past few years has really kept manufacturers on their toes, and there is now a better range of cake decorations more widely available than ever before. At first glance, the majority of plastic and fabric decorations may look cheap and very artificial, but with a little thought given to their application and indeed probably some modification or adaptation, you can make great use of anything from plastic lettering, numerals and bells to fabric butterflies, flowers and leaves. The secret is not to use the items as they are straight from the pack – tweak the flowers, curve the leaves, trim the lettering to suit and then attach them to your cake and you'll be surprised at the difference! Fabric, wafer and piped icing flowers, all available commercially, will benefit from a quick tint with dusting powder, just to make them more individual. Writing on cakes is usually the most difficult part so take advantage of the many cut out letters, numbers and popular inscriptions that are available, and don't forget ribbons, bows and cake candles – birthday cakes aren't the same without colourful ribbon trimmings and candles to blow out. If you think sticking candles in your cake will spoil the look of it, insert them just before the party.

Edible decorations are becoming increasingly popular and you can now obtain everything from lettering and hand-made flowers to printed plaques and ready-made icing in tubes.

There is a wide range of bought plastic lettering available.

The design and quality of plastic decorations has improved considerably. There is now also a greater range of fabric flowers, leaves, beads and ribbons to choose from.

PREPARING THE CAKE

Preparing the cake is a most important part of cake decorating work. Careful handling, cutting and neat layering all contribute to making an accurate cake base on which to build and they also provide a visually pleasing appearance to the cake when cut.

SPONGE CAKES

Ideally freshly baked cakes should be stored (not refrigerated) for approximately 12 hours before beginning work with them. It is particularly important to store them before cutting. When the cake has cooled, wrap it loosely in a polythene sheet. This storage period allows the crumb to close a little and the cake as a whole to firm up, thus enabling easier handling. Ready-made shop-bought cake bases do not require a firming period and can be used straight away. Frozen cakes can be used immediately they have defrosted, although if you have any intricate cutting to do, do this before the cake has fully defrosted as the firmness will make it easier to produce a neater shape. Before cutting, layering or masking of any kind, remove the thin crust or 'skin' of the cake by drawing the back edge of a long knife across the cake. Alternatively, use a sharp serrated knife in a conventional manner. Having prepared the cake, you can then spread the top and sides with buttercream or jam before covering with sugarpaste.

FRUIT CAKES

Prepare these in the conventional manner by first moistening and flavouring with a brushing of brandy or rum. Cover the cake's top and sides with a layer of almond marzipan, attaching it to the cake with boiled apricot jam to act as an adhesive. To cover the cake with sugarpaste, follow the method opposite but instead of attaching the sugarpaste with buttercream or jam, simply brush the marzipan covering with a little gin or vodka.

Prepare fruit cakes in the conventional manner, covering top and sides with a layer of almond marzipan. To stick the sugarpaste on, brush the marzipan lightly with alcohol.

QUICK-TO-DO CAKE COVERING

The sugarpaste referred to in each recipe for covering the cakes and boards is commercially available in a ready-to-roll form. The paste can be bought either in white, which allows you to produce your own colours, or ready-coloured in a limited but popular range of tints.

COLOURING SUGARPASTE

To colour the paste, simply add the desired colouring. Paste colours give the best results and you can obtain strong colours without softening the paste, as would be the result if liquid colours were used. Add the colouring to the sugarpaste using a cocktail stick (toothpick) and knead thoroughly until evenly distributed. While you are working and in particular during storage, keep any unused paste covered with polythene to prevent it drying out.

CAKES

Having coloured the paste, it is ready to roll out. If you are using white paste, it will require a short kneading time to soften it and make it more pliable. Prepare the cake by covering with a thin spreading of buttercream or jam to act as an adhesive for the sugarpaste. Roll out sugarpaste on a flat, clean surface such as a kitchen worktop or a large cutting

board dusted with icing (confectioner's) sugar. Pick up the paste by sliding your hands, palms uppermost, underneath it and lifting it onto the cake. Carefully remove your hands, allowing the paste to drape loosely over the cake. Slightly curve one hand and tease the paste smoothly over the cake, removing any creases and folds as you go. Trim off any excess paste from the base using a small knife, then use a smoother or flat plastic scraper to make a clean, neat, flawless surface. Set the cake aside or transfer onto a cake board ready for decoration. The technique is basically the same for all shapes of cakes, although with some of the more intricate shapes, such as petal and hexagon, it may take more time to achieve a good finish.

Pick up the sugarpaste by sliding your hands underneath and lift onto the cake. Drape the paste loosely on the cake and smooth from the centre to remove any air pockets.

Having cut and layered the cake with cream and/or jam and removed any unwanted crust, spread the cake top and sides with a thin layer of apricot jam, ready for covering in sugarpaste.

After removing creases and folds, use a small knife to trim excess paste from the base.

If you prefer the flavour or handling qualities of buttercream instead of jam, it will still do the same job of acting as an adhesive to stick the sugarpaste to the cake.

Use a smoother or flat plastic scraper to create a clean, neat, flawless surface. Smoothing needs to be done immediately after covering and before the paste skins.

Prepare the cake board by brushing with water to make the sugarpaste stick. Don't wet the board, simply moisten it, otherwise the paste will slide and slip rather than stick.

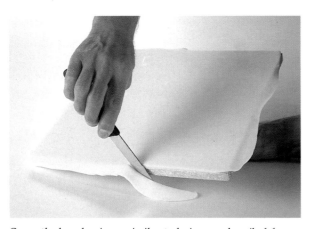

Cover the board using a similar technique as described for covering the cake. Smooth the surface to remove any air pockets and neatly trim the edges with a small knife.

The covered board can be left as it is, but for a more decorative finish use a crimping tool whilst the paste is still soft to create a fancy border around the edge.

CAKE BOARDS

Covering cake boards with sugarpaste uses the same method as described for cakes (see page 45), except the cake board is lightly moistened with water to make the sugarpaste adhere. Trim off excess sugarpaste using a small knife. The board can be covered fully or you may prefer to make a template of the cake shape and cut away this area of sugarpaste before placing the cake on the board, securing it with dabs of royal icing. If the board edge is to be decorated with a crimping tool, this should be done while the sugarpaste is still soft. To give a more finished look to your cakes, attach a suitably coloured ribbon or silver or gold paper banding to the board edge at the last stage of decoration.

COLOURINGS

A wider variety of edible food colourings than ever before is now available, in liquid and paste form, powder and pens.

LIQUID COLOUR

Liquid colour has previously been restricted to being suitable mainly for producing pastel tints. If using such a weak colour solution, avoid trying to produce very dark shades as the amount of liquid required usually renders the royal icing (or sugarpaste) too soft to work with.

PASTE COLOUR

Available in a comprehensive range of colours, these are regarded as the best to use for colouring sugarpaste and royal icing. Use the tip of a cocktail stick (toothpick) to add the colour in small amounts until the desired tint or shade is produced.

DUSTING POWDER

This type, as the name implies, is mainly used in novelty cake work for dusting colour onto sugarpaste to create interesting effects. It is also used to tint leaves and the centres or petal edges of flowers. It can be used to colour royal icing, but as the intensity is not very strong it is uneconomical to use in large quantities.

ROYAL ICING

Used mainly for piping lettering and linework and for attaching decorations to cakes.

15g (½oz) albumen powder or albumen-based powder
90ml (3fl oz/⅓ cup) water
500g (1lb/4 cups) icing (confectioner's) sugar, finely sieved

Prepare the albumen powder with water according to the manufacturer's instructions. Strain the solution into a bowl. Add half the sugar, mixing well with a wooden spatula or spoon. Add the remaining sugar and continue mixing until all the icing sugar is incorporated. Scrape down the sides of the bowl, then lightly beat the mixture by hand or electric mixer until a definite bold peak is left when a spoonful of mixture is lifted from the bowl with a spatula. Store the icing in an airtight container until required. When in use, cover the bowl with a clean, moist cloth to prevent the icing crusting.

BUTTERCREAM

Used to sandwich cakes together, with or without a layer of jam. Buttercream, instead of jam, can also be spread thinly onto cakes as an adhesive medium for the sugarpaste covering.

185g (6oz/¾ cup) butter, softened
2 tbsp milk
375g (12oz/3 cups) icing (confectioner's) sugar
few drops of vanilla essence, to taste

Place the softened butter in a large bowl. Gradually add the milk, working the mixture together until creamy. For a less rich filling, a combination of soft butter and a quality margarine may be used, in which case less liquid will be required.

Sift the icing (confectioner's) sugar and gradually stir into the butter and milk mixture, then beat hard with a wooden spoon or electric mixer until pale, light and fluffy. A little extra liquid may be needed if a soft icing is required. Flavour as desired, with vanilla essence.

TRUFFLE PASTE

A firm paste ideal for moulding and shaping, this is particularly useful for difficult-to-shape pieces.

500g (1lb/8 cups) cake crumbs (see Note)
60g (2oz/⅓ cup) apricot jam
60ml (2fl oz/¼ cup) evaporated milk
½ tsp vanilla essence
about 125g (4oz) melted chocolate (see Note)

Place cake crumbs in bowl, add jam, evaporated milk and vanilla essence. Mix using a spoon then stream in melted chocolate and continue mixing until a firm paste is formed – a dry mix will crumble and be difficult to mould, while a mixture that is too soft will not retain its shape.

The prepared mixture will keep for a few days sealed in an airtight container in a refrigerator. To create shapes, simply mould using your hands dusted with icing (confectioner's) sugar. Attach shaped pieces to the main cake using jam, melted chocolate or buttercream.

Note If using chocolate cake crumbs, use milk or plain chocolate. For plain cake crumbs, use white chocolate. The amount of chocolate required varies depending whether the crumbs are dry or moist.

Truffle paste makes use of leftover cake trimmings which can be frozen in polythene bags. Freeze whole if to be used for forming shapes or crumb and sieve them for making truffle paste.

PREPARING TO DECORATE

In the following recipes, if a sponge cake has been used, the quantity of buttercream or jam for filling and masking (covering) the cake is your choice. For the filling, it is personal taste whether you like one layer of jam or buttercream or you may like to split the cake twice and fill with a layer of each to add colour and flavour. Jam and buttercream also do the same job of sticking the sugarpaste to the cake.

For the majority of recipes you will need a small amount of either water or reconstituted egg white powder or similar substitute for attaching various off-pieces and decorations to the main cake. For application use an appropriately sized brush.

BIRTHDAY EXPRESS
WHEELS TEMPLATE PAGE 17

WHEELS TEMPLATE

Edited by Gillian Haslam
Designed by Christine Wood
Photography by Clive Streeter

Published 1994 by Merehurst Limited

Distributed by J.B. Fairfax Press Ltd
9 Trinity Centre, Park Farm
Wellingborough, Northamptonshire
NN8 6ZB

Copyright © Merehurst Limited 1994

A catalogue record for this book is available from the
British Library
ISBN 1–874567–60–3

Typeset by J&L Composition Ltd, UK
Colour separation by Fotographics Ltd, UK–Hong Kong
Printed in Italy by G. Canale & C., S.p.A.

ACKNOWLEDGEMENTS

Cake Art Ltd, Venture Way, Crown Estate,
Priorswood, Taunton, Somerset TA2 8DE

Filtering Media Manufacturers, Unit 5, Kings Park,
Primrose Hill, Kings Langley, Herts WD4 8ST

G. T. Culpitt & Son Ltd, Culpitt House, Place Farm,
Wheathampstead, Herts AL4 8SB

Guy Paul & Co Ltd, Unit B4, Foundry Way, Little
End Road, Eaton Socon, Cambs PE19 3JH

J. F. Renshaw Ltd, Mitcham House, River Court,
Albert Drive, Woking, Surrey GU21 5RP

Squires Kitchen, Squires House, 3 Waverley Lane,
Farnham, Surrey GU9 8BB

The Icing Shop, 259A Orrell Road, Orrell, Wigan
WN5 8NB

THE GREAT BIBLE DISCOVERY

THE PROMISE

THE BIBLE IS A BEST-SELLER. IT IS ALSO ONE OF THE MASTER-WORKS OF WORLD LITERATURE - SO IMPORTANT THAT UNIVERSITIES TODAY TEACH 'NON-RELIGIOUS' BIBLE COURSES TO HELP STUDENTS WHO CHOOSE TO STUDY WESTERN LITERATURE.

THE BIBLE POSSESSES AN AMAZING POWER TO FASCINATE YOUNG AND OLD ALIKE.

ONE REASON FOR THIS UNIVERSAL APPEAL IS THAT IT DEALS WITH BASIC HUMAN LONGINGS, EMOTIONS, RELATIONSHIPS. 'ALL THE WORLD IS HERE.' ANOTHER REASON IS THAT SO MUCH OF THE BIBLE CONSISTS OF STORIES. THEY ARE FULL OF MEANING BUT EASY TO REMEMBER.

HERE ARE THOSE STORIES, PRESENTED SIMPLY AND WITH A MINIMUM OF EXPLANATION. WE HAVE LEFT THE TEXT TO SPEAK FOR ITSELF. GIFTED ARTISTS USE THE ACTION-STRIP TECHNIQUE TO BRING THE BIBLE'S DEEP MESSAGE TO READERS OF ALL AGES. THEIR DRAWINGS ARE BASED ON INFORMATION FROM ARCHAEOLOGICAL DISCOVERIES COVERING FIFTEEN CENTURIES.

AN ANCIENT BOOK - PRESENTED FOR THE PEOPLE OF THE SECOND MILLENNIUM. A RELIGIOUS BOOK - PRESENTED FREE FROM THE INTERPRETATION OF ANY PARTICULAR CHURCH. A UNIVERSAL BOOK - PRESENTED IN A FORM THAT ALL MAY ENJOY.

M publishing
CARLISLE, UK

2

When Abraham left Ur, God promised that his descendants would be a great nation. After he had reached Canaan, a homeless wanderer, God made another promise: one day the land would belong to Abraham's children.

The story of Abraham, his son Isaac and his son Jacob, is a story of promises. How amazing that God should humble himself by making promises to humankind and bind himself by a covenant! It's not even as if the men and women concerned were wonderfully virtuous. The slave Hagar was first used to provide Abraham with the heir Sarah failed to produce and then thrown out of the 'family'. Jacob deceived his own father in order to secure the first-born's right to the blessings of the promise.

But Esau, who suffered from Jacob's sharp practice, showed in other ways that he did not value God's promise. Jacob, by contrast (and his mother Rebekah), took God and the promise seriously throughout his life. So did Abraham, who was even willing to sacrifice the son on whom he depended if God were to keep the promise of descendants. On this occasion his faith rose to the challenge, as it had when he had given his nephew Lot the right to the best land. (This was before the devastation of the area around what we now call the 'Dead' Sea.)

The way in which the stories are told is remarkably free from moral judgements. The Bible often records violent and immoral behaviour with little comment, if any. In the same way, it is often content merely to describe brave and faithful conduct. Readers are often left to draw their own conclusions - or ask their own questions. Sometimes we can see wrongdoing reaping its own harvest, as when Jacob, the deceiver, was cheated by his Uncle Laban. But by no means always.

The illustrations in this series are based on accurate research into the way buildings and clothes changed according to time and place, from Egypt and Mesopotamia and finally into the worlds of Greece and Rome. These changes may also remind us that the men and women in these stories inhabited a different world from ours. God was the same, of course. But they thought of him in their way, not ours.

Genesis 12 - 36

2

THE PROMISE

First published as *Découvrir la Bible* 1983

First edition © Librairie Larousse 1983
English translation © Daan Retief Publishers 1990
24-volume series adaptation by Mike Jacklin © Knowledge Unlimited 1994
This edition © OM Publishing 1995

01 00 99 98 97 96 95   7 6 5 4 3 2 1

OM Publishing is an imprint of Send the Light Ltd.,
P.O. Box 300, Carlisle, Cumbria CA3 0QS, U.K.

Series editor: D. Roy Briggs
English translation: Bethan Uden
Introductions: Peter Cousins

British Library Cataloguing in Publication Data
A catalogue record for this book is available from the British Library
ISBN 1-85078-206-7

Printed in Singapore by Tien Wah Press (Pte) Ltd.

ABRAHAM
part 2

WHILE HE WAS AT THE OAKS OF MAMRE, ABRAHAM WAS VISITED BY THREE MESSENGERS. THEY WERE VERY ANGRY WITH SODOM. WHEN ABRAHAM DEFENDED THE TOWN, THEY MADE THIS AGREEMENT WITH HIM: IF THEY FOUND TEN GOOD PEOPLE IN SODOM, THEY WOULD NOT DESTROY IT. TWO OF THEM TRAVELLED TO SODOM.

OUTSIDE THE WALLS OF SODOM LOT WAS ENJOYING THE PEACE OF THE EVENING...

...WHEN THE TWO MESSENGERS ARRIVED...

SIRS, DO ME THE HONOUR OF SPENDING THE NIGHT IN MY HOUSE.

LET'S GO THIS WAY. IT'S MORE SECLUDED.

STORY: Etienne DAHLER.   DRAWING: Victor de la FUENTE

3

LOT SPOKE AT LENGTH ABOUT THE SIN OF SODOM.

MY BROTHERS, CALM DOWN. TAKE MY TWO DAUGHTERS, BUT DON'T TOUCH MY GUESTS.

LET'S GET LOT!

LET US PASS!

HE CAME AS A STRANGER AND NOW HE WANTS TO BE THE JUDGE!

THEY'VE ADOPTED SIN AS THEIR LAW. THEY CAN'T REPENT ANY LONGER...

DON'T WORRY, LOT. THEY'LL NOT GET IN.

WAKE UP YOUR FAMILY. YOU MUST FLEE!

WE'RE GOING TO DESTROY THIS PLACE.

THE EARTH
BEGAN TO SHAKE.

NOTHING COULD
BE DONE. EVEN
HIS FUTURE SONS-
IN-LAW WOULDN'T
GO WITH HIM.

LOT'S WIFE STOPPED ON THE WAY, AND
BECAME A PILLAR OF SALT.

FOR LOVE OF HIS
UNCLE, ABRAHAM,
GOD SAVED LOT.

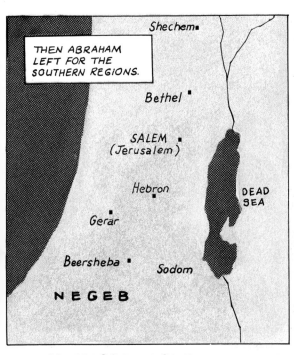

THEN ABRAHAM LEFT FOR THE SOUTHERN REGIONS.

ARRIVING AMONGST THE PHILISTINES, ABRAHAM AGAIN LET IT BE KNOWN THAT SARAH WAS HIS SISTER. IN ALL GOOD FAITH...

... **ABIMELECH,** THE PHILISTINE KING, CARRIED HER OFF.

THE FOLLOWING NIGHT IN A DREAM...

ABIMELECH, YOU'LL DIE, BECAUSE THIS WOMAN HAS A HUSBAND.

I DIDN'T KNOW. I ACTED WITH A PURE HEART.

GIVE HER BACK TO ABRAHAM.

* ISAAC

THE YEARS PASSED...

WHAT A GRAND FEAST IN HONOUR OF YOUR SON!

YES. BUT... SARAH, WHERE'S ISAAC? HAVE HIM BROUGHT HERE.

HE MUST BE PLAYING WITH THE OTHER CHILDREN. I'LL CALL HIM.

ISAAC!

ISHMAEL'S ALWAYS MISTREATING ISAAC... SO SEND AWAY THIS SLAVE-WOMAN AND HER SON...

...AND MY SON.

I WILL ALSO MAKE A NATION FROM THE SON OF YOUR SLAVE, BUT THE DESCENDANTS BEARING YOUR NAME WILL COME FROM ISAAC.

THE NEXT DAY, HAGAR...

ABRAHAM, THAT'S **IMPOSSIBLE!**

YOUR SON'S HAD A FEVER SINCE YESTERDAY.

GO, HAGAR! IT MUST BE...

...LEAVE YOUR COUNTRY, YOUR FAMILY, AND THE HOUSE OF YOUR FATHER, AND GO TO THE LAND I WILL SHOW YOU.

HAGAR WALKED FOR MANY HOURS. SHE GOT LOST. THE SUN BLINDED HER. HER WATERSKIN WAS EMPTY.

ISHMAEL, I'M SURE WE'LL FIND A WATER-HOLE.

I DON'T WANT TO SEE MY CHILD DIE!

I... I'M THIRSTY... FATHER...!

ISHMAEL'S CRY WAS HEARD...

GE

YOU'LL FIND A SPRING A FEW KILOMETRES TO THE WEST.

THEY WENT TO LIVE IN THE ARABIAN DESERT...

ISHMAEL HAD TWELVE SONS:
NEBAIOTH, KEDAR, ADBEEL, MIBSAM, MISHMA, DUMAH, MASSA, HADAD, TEMAN, JETUR, NAPHISH, KEDEMAH.

NOW, AS A POTTER TESTS HIS POTS, KEEPING THE GOOD AND BREAKING THE FAULTY ONES, GOD ONCE MORE TESTED ABRAHAM.

TAKE YOUR SON, ISAAC, THE ONE YOU LOVE; GO TO THE LAND OF MORIAH, AND OFFER HIM AS A SACRIFICE ON THE MOUNTAIN I WILL SHOW YOU.

WHY DOES GOD ASK SUCH A THING OF ME...

...I WHO HAVE ALWAYS CONDEMNED THE IDOLATORS FOR THEIR HUMAN SACRIFICES...

FATHER, I CAN GO INSTEAD OF YOU...

ABRAHAM CAN'T GO...

KEEP GOING! WE'RE NEARLY THERE!

...BUT NEVERTHELESS GOD HAS SAID: 'YOUR DESCENDANTS WILL COME FROM ISAAC.'

AFTER WALKING FOR THREE DAYS, ABRAHAM SCANNED THE HORIZON...

STAY HERE WITH THE DONKEY. ISAAC, YOU CARRY THE WOOD FOR THE SACRIFICE.

CAN YOU SEE ANYTHING OVER THERE?

NO, MASTER.

FATHER, WE HAVE THE FIRE AND THE WOOD, BUT WHERE'S THE LAMB?

GOD HIMSELF WILL PROVIDE THE LAMB FOR THE SACRIFICE.

THEN ABRAHAM SAW A RAM AND OFFERED IT ON THE FIRE INSTEAD OF HIS SON.

SARAH'S **JUST DIED.** GO QUICKLY AND TELL THE MASTER IN BEERSHEBA.

AT HEBRON, A LITTLE LATER...

I WANT A PLACE TO BURY **SARAH.**

TO THE LEADING MEN OF HEBRON...

ABRAHAM, YOU'RE A LEADER FROM GOD AMONGST US. CHOOSE ONE OF OUR TOMBS.

THE PATRIARCH ASKED FOR THE CAVE OF MACHPELAH. HE BOUGHT IT: **THE FIRST PIECE OF THE PROMISED LAND.**

BY THIS ACT I GIVE ALL MY BELONGINGS TO ISAAC. BUT REMEMBER, HE MUST NEVER LEAVE **THE PROMISED LAND.**

MY MASTER, I SWEAR IT TO YOU!'

COME BACK QUICKLY! ...OTHERWISE I'LL NEVER KNOW HER...

HARAN

Euphrates

Mediterranean

BEERSHEBA
HEBRON

HEBRON–HARAN: ABOUT 30 DAYS ON FOOT.

WE'RE APPROACHING HARAN. LET'S LOOK FOR A WATER - HOLE THAT'S THE PLACE TO HEAR THE LATEST NEWS.

NEAR THE WELL, ELIEZER ASKS THE LORD FOR A SIGN.

WILL I FIND HER HERE?... **AND HOW WILL I RECOGNIZE HER?**

LORD, GOD OF ABRAHAM ... THE YOUNG GIRL TO WHOM I SAY 'LOWER YOUR JAR TO LET ME DRINK...'

AND WHO REPLIES 'DRINK, AND I'LL WATER YOUR CAMELS TOO...'

...LET HER BE THE BRIDE YOU'VE DESTINED FOR ISAAC.

LOOK, HERE'S REBECCA!

...SHE'S COME TO GET WATER...

AND THE SIGN HE'D ASKED FOR CAME TRUE.

BLESSED BE THE ETERNAL GOD WHO BROUGHT ME RIGHT TO MY MASTER'S FAMILY...!

REBECCA RAN HOME TO TELL THEM ABOUT HER MEETING...

I'M LABAN, BROTHER OF REBECCA WHO GAVE YOU A DRINK. DON'T PITCH YOUR TENT! COME TO OUR HOME...

SPEAK!

IN HIS TURN, ELIEZER TOLD HIS STORY BETHUEL, THE YOUNG GIRL'S FATHER, LISTENED TO HIM.

ALL THIS COMES FROM GOD. LET REBECCA BE THE WIFE OF YOUR MASTER'S SON.

DO YOU AGREE TO GO WITH THIS MAN, REBECCA?

YES FATHER. I COULD LEAVE TOMORROW.

HERE ARE PRESENTS FROM MY MASTER.

GOOD! NOW LET'S EAT!

SARAH'S DEATH HAD
SADDENED ISAAC.
BUT THAT EVENING...

BACK
ALREADY?

STOP!

A MAN IN THE
DISTANCE. HE'S
COMING THIS WAY. HE'S
RUNNING. ISN'T HE THE
SON OF YOUR
MASTER?

YES!
IT'S ISAAC!

THIS IS REBECCA,
THE DAUGHTER
OF BETHUEL.

MY
LORD!

REBECCA, YOU'VE BEEN FOUND WORTHY TO GIVE ABRAHAM HEIRS.

REBECCA WILL BE THE MOTHER OF THOUSANDS...

NOW I CAN PEACEFULLY GO TO BE WITH SARAH. EVERYTHING'S YOURS, ISAAC... *AND ALSO THE PROMISE GOD GAVE ME.*

THE WEDDING OF ISAAC AND REBECCA CAUSED GREAT JOY IN THE HOUSE OF ABRAHAM.

TEACH YOUR CHILDREN THESE THINGS. MAKE SURE THEY FAITHFULLY SERVE THE MOST HIGH.

SO THE YEARS WENT BY.

ISAAC PRAYED SILENTLY. HE HAD NO CHILDREN.

THE CHILDREN GREW UP.
ESAU BECAME A SKILLED AND
CUNNING HUNTER.
JACOB WAS A QUIET MAN,
WHO SPENT HIS DAYS
AROUND THE TENTS.

MY GOD,
YOU'VE BLESSED ME
FAR BEYOND
MY HOPES.

THEN, AT A GREAT AGE, ABRAHAM DIED...

HIS SONS AND
GRANDSONS CARRIED
HIM TO THE CAVE OF
MACHPELAH, WHERE
SARAH WAS BURIED.

ISHMAEL,
LET'S NEVER FORGET
THAT HE WAS FATHER
TO BOTH OF US.

YES, ISAAC,
OUR DESCENDANTS
MUST ALWAYS
REMEMBER
THAT!

THERE WAS A FAMINE IN CANAAN, LIKE THAT IN THE TIME OF ABRAHAM.

FOLLOWING THE EXAMPLE OF HIS FATHER, ISAAC DECIDED TO BREAK CAMP AND GO TO EGYPT.

DO NOT GO DOWN INTO EGYPT. STAY IN THIS LAND. I WILL BE WITH YOU AND I WILL KEEP THE PROMISE MADE TO YOUR FATHER ABRAHAM.

ISAAC OBEYED... HE STAYED IN CANAAN...

AFTER ENDLESS DAYS OF UNBEARABLE DROUGHT, THE RAIN CAME TO GIVE HIS PEOPLE LIFE.

...AND FORTUNE SMILED ON HIM. HE HARVESTED 100 TIMES MORE THAN HE HAD SOWN.

... RICHER THAN ALL OF US PUT TOGETHER. HE TAKES OUR LAND AND THE WATER FROM OUR SPRINGS. ARE WE GOING TO LET HIM **HAVE THE WHOLE COUNTRY?**

THE PEOPLE OF THE COUNTRY ARE JEALOUS OF ISAAC'S SUCCESS.

... THE THIRD WELL WE'VE FILLED IN SINCE THIS MORNING...

HIS REACTION WILL BE TERRIBLE ...

MASTER, WE'RE THE STRONGEST. ONE WORD FROM YOU AND THEY'RE IN OUR HANDS.

NO! LET'S WITHDRAW AND WAIT UNTIL THEIR ANGER'S DIED DOWN.

THE NEWS WAS TAKEN TO ISAAC...

ISAAC LEFT THERE, CAMPING IN THE VALLEY OF GERAR. THEN HE MOVED TO BEERSHEBA...

... AND SETTLED THERE. THEY SET ABOUT DIGGING A WELL. ONE DAY ISAAC SAW ABIMELECH, THE KING, COMING TOWARDS HIM. HE HAD LEFT GERAR, ACCOMPANIED BY PHICOL, THE COMMANDER OF HIS ARMY.

WHY COME TO ME, IF YOU HATE ME? YOU CHASED ME OUT OF YOUR COUNTRY...

IT'S PLAIN TO US THAT GOD'S WITH YOU, ISAAC. **WE'VE COME TO MAKE PEACE WITH YOU.**

AND THEY SWORE AN OATH. THE NEXT DAY, ABIMELCH HAD JUST GONE, WHEN...

...THE WELL... IT'S HERE, MASTER! WATER! AT SHIBAH...! *

* The name means 'oath'.

29

AFTER THAT ISAAC LIVED PEACEFULLY AT BEERSHEBA.

ESAU, HIS SON, MARRIED TWO HITTITE GIRLS, JUDITH AND BASEMATH.

IN HIS OLD AGE ISAAC BECAME BLIND. ONE DAY HE CALLED ESAU...

MY SON, I'M GOING TO DIE SOON... GO HUNTING AND PREPARE ME A DISH OF VENISON. **I'LL GIVE YOU MY BLESSING AS THE FIRST-BORN.**

YOU MUST ACT QUICKLY, JACOB! YOUR FATHER'S GOING TO BLESS ESAU; THEN THERE'LL BE NOTHING MORE WE CAN DO.

BUT REBECCA OVERHEARD.

GO AND GET ME TWO GOATS FROM THE HERD. I'LL MAKE ONE OF YOUR FATHER'S FAVOURITE DISHES.

JACOB OBEYED.

30

REBECCA TOOK A GOATSKIN...

31

34

36

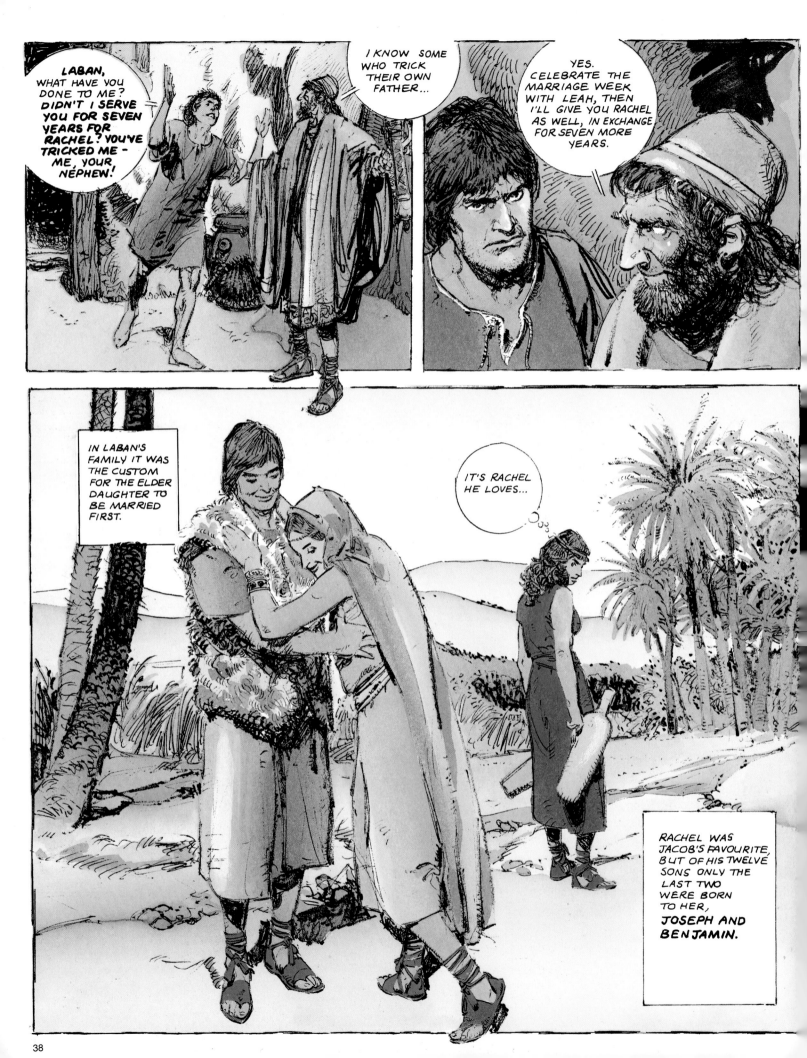

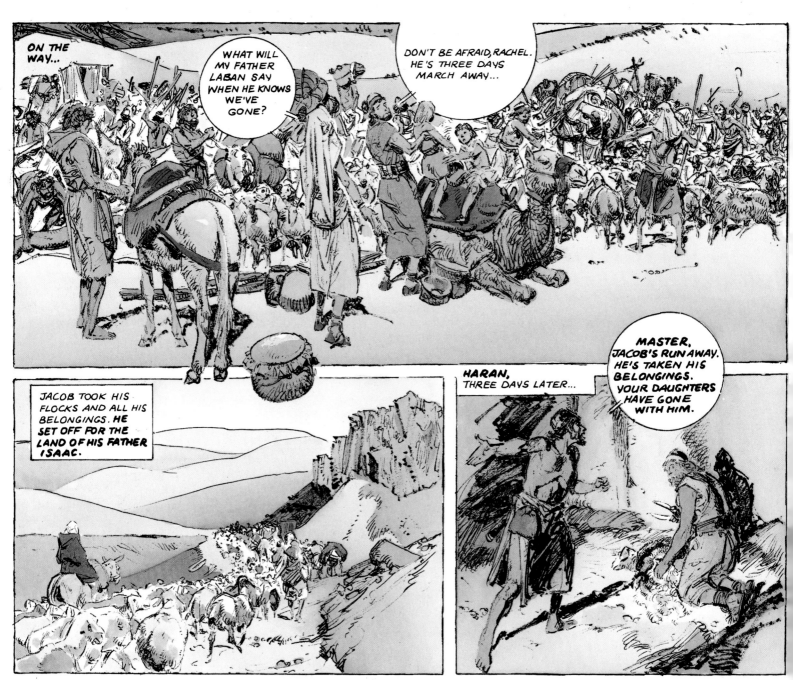

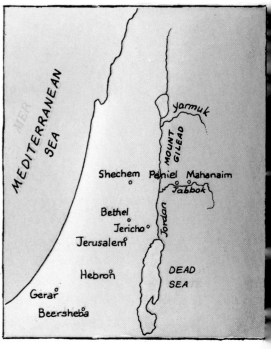

41

JACOB WANTED TO MAKE A DETOUR THROUGH EDOM TO THE BANKS OF THE JABBOK.

I MUST STILL MAKE PEACE WITH MY BROTHER.

PITCHING HIS CAMP AT MAHANAIM, JACOB SENT A MESSENGER TO THE LAND OF EDOM.

KEEP THE FLOCKS APART, AND GO TO MEET ESAU. OFFER HIM THESE FLOCKS TO APPEASE HIS ANGER.

AS A RESULT...

ESAU'S MARCHING TOWARDS YOU WITH 400 MEN!

WE'LL SPLIT INTO TWO CAMPS* IF ONE'S ATTACKED, THE OTHER MAY BE ABLE TO ESCAPE.

GOD OF MY FATHER ISAAC! YOU TOLD ME TO COME BACK TO CANAAN; NOW DELIVER ME FROM THE HAND OF ESAU.

IT GREW DARK...

* Mahanaim means 'the two camps'.

ALONE AT THE FORD OF JABBOK...

... SOMEONE WRESTLED WITH HIM UNTIL DAYBREAK...

LET ME GO; IT'S GETTING LIGHT.

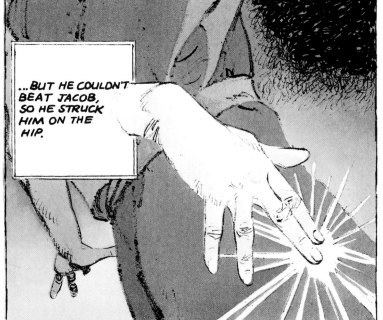

...BUT HE COULDN'T BEAT JACOB, SO HE STRUCK HIM ON THE HIP.

YOU SHAN'T GO WITHOUT BLESSING ME!

45

JACOB SETTLED AT SHECHEM FOR MANY YEARS.

LET'S GO TO BETHEL AND THANK THE LORD THAT WE LIVE IN PEACE.

BUT FIRST GET RID OF YOUR FOREIGN GODS. WE MUST PURIFY OURSELVES!

JACOB BURIED ALL THE IDOLS UNDER THE OAK-TREE NEAR SHECHEM. THEN HE SET OFF...

...FOR BETHEL. THERE GOD HAD APPEARED TO HIM IN A DREAM IN HIS YOUTH, AND GIVEN HIM A PROMISE...

I WILL GIVE YOU THE LAND I PROMISED TO ABRAHAM AND ISAAC, AND I WILL GIVE IT TO YOUR DESCENDANTS AFTER YOU.

THE CARAVAN SET OFF AGAIN. NEAR TO RAMAH, RACHEL FELT THE FIRST PANGS OF CHILDBIRTH.

STOP! MY MISTRESS RACHEL'S PAINS HAVE BEGUN!

A CHILD WAS BORN. A SON. BUT RACHEL DIED.

IN MEMORY OF HER WHO WAS MY STRENGTH, MY LIGHT, MY JOY, I'LL CALL YOU BENJAMIN.*

*In Hebrew; SON OF GOOD FORTUNE.

AT LAST JACOB REACHED HEBRON. HE FOUND ISAAC, BUT HIS MOTHER REBECCA HAD DIED.

MY SON! AFTER SO MANY YEARS... I FEARED I'D NEVER SEE YOU AGAIN.

A FEW YEARS LATER THE OLD MAN ALSO DIED.

THE LORD IS OUR GOD; HIS COMMANDS ARE FOR ALL THE WORLD. HE WILL KEEP HIS COVENANT FOREVER, HIS PROMISES FOR A THOUSAND GENERATIONS. HE WILL KEEP THE AGREEMENT HE MADE WITH ABRAHAM AND HIS PROMISE TO ISAAC. THE LORD MADE A COVENANT WITH JACOB, ONE THAT WILL LAST FOREVER.

Psalm 105